be still
and know
that
I AM
GOD
I WILL BE EXALTED

SHER PAI

FLYING ARROW
MINISTRIES
FLYINGARROWMINISTRIES.COM

CONTENTS

INTRODUCTION

God's great pleasure is relationship with His children. He knows how easily we can be overcome and distracted with fear, anxiety and worry when trouble draws near. He is at work so we can rest. He provides powerful reminders of His constant presence, His diligent care, and His limitless ability to help. His desire is for unbroken communion between Him and His children. He opens our spiritual eyes of faith in the midst of trouble to see that we are faithfully preserved and kept in the secret refuge of God, safely supplied in the shadow of the Almighty. He spreads His feathers over us and we are provided a place in Christ to be still, let go and intimately commune with Him.

Psalm forty-six is a celebration song of the many victories God won for His people. Within the lyrics God provided a template for maintaining the peace, joy and rest He had supplied through those victories over enemy nations. God's very presence was with them in the land He provided. His people needed only to recognize Who He is, remember His past blessings, receive His promises of help, and rest in the shadow of His presence.

This study is designed to help cultivate the habit of responding to trouble in a way that pleases God and keeps us spiritually thriving. Located at the end of each chapter is a RECOGNIZE, REMEMBER, RECEIVE, REST section. Take time each week to thoughtfully respond to God and develop the habit of acknowledging His presence.

RECOGNIZE

Recognize God in the midst of trouble. Acknowledge God's character and attributes. List the things you learn during the week about who God is and what He is able to do. You can refer to the names of God and His attributes on the inside of the front cover.

REMEMBER

Take time to recall and record the many blessings and benefits God has provided for you during the week.

RECEIVE

Research and respond in faith to the promises God has given you through His Word. Record the promises God has given to you during the week. You can reference some of His promises on the back inside cover.

REST

Choose to let go of the things that are disturbing your peace and joy. Record what you will release into the Almighty loving hands of God.

PSALM 46

GOD IS OUR REFUGE AND STRENGTH,
A VERY PRESENT HELP IN TROUBLE.
THEREFORE WE WILL NOT FEAR, EVEN THOUGH THE EARTH BE REMOVED,
AND THOUGH THE MOUNTAINS BE CARRIED INTO THE MIDST OF THE SEA;
THOUGH ITS WATERS ROAR AND BE TROUBLED,
THOUGH THE MOUNTAINS SHAKE WITH ITS SWELLING. SELAH
THERE IS A RIVER WHOSE STREAMS SHALL MAKE GLAD THE CITY OF GOD,
THE HOLY PLACE OF THE TABERNACLE OF THE MOST HIGH.
GOD IS IN THE MIDST OF HER, SHE SHALL NOT BE MOVED;
GOD SHALL HELP HER, JUST AT THE BREAK OF DAWN.
THE NATIONS RAGED, THE KINGDOMS WERE MOVED;
HE UTTERED HIS VOICE, THE EARTH MELTED.
THE LORD OF HOSTS IS WITH US;
THE GOD OF JACOB IS OUR REFUGE. SELAH
COME, BEHOLD THE WORKS OF THE LORD,
WHO HAS MADE DESOLATIONS IN THE EARTH.
HE MAKES WARS CEASE TO THE END OF THE EARTH;
HE BREAKS THE BOW AND CUTS THE SPEAR IN TWO;
HE BURNS THE CHARIOT IN THE FIRE.
BE STILL, AND KNOW THAT I AM GOD;
I WILL BE EXALTED AMONG THE NATIONS, I WILL BE EXALTED IN THE EARTH!
THE LORD OF HOSTS IS WITH US; THE GOD OF JACOB IS OUR REFUGE.
SELAH

CHAPTER

1

BE STILL AND KNOW THAT I AM GOD

Living out a day to day life of calm confidence in God's promises and plans is much easier studied than done! All of us desire to experience and exhibit a peaceful and joyful trust in our God who is both good and faithful. But a single day can hold a myriad of circumstances that can whip up fear, disturb our peace and take us down with anxiety. What often starts out well, as we rise from a quiet time with God—saturated with reminders of His character, and encouragement to trust Him today—does not end up as well as we had hoped. Our hearts sometimes sink heavily upon our beds, weighed down with cares and concerns, restless as we wrestle to let go and trust God.

It is believed that Psalm 46 was written as a celebration song to commemorate the many victories God had won for King David and the Israelites. It surely became not only a victory song but a song that would stir up a remembrance of God's past protection, presence, and help when the threats of new enemy nations reached their ears. It is comforting to see that God not only provided a present place of rest but also a pattern for maintaining the peace of mind and joy of heart that the victories had achieved for His children.

God wanted His people to remember that He had been their refuge, the One to whom they could flee and hide when danger drew near. He had been their strength, the One who used His unlimited power to protect and preserve them. He had been a very present help in their times of trouble. He had been a constant; a great and abundant force for them—found sufficient, proven to be a diligent aid, assisting them in their distress and tribulation.

Therefore, in their present adversity they can count on His very present help! Though the earth be removed and the mountains be carried into the midst of the sea; when earthly help crumbles and all senses tell them that there is no hope, that is when they are to remember God's past aid and confidently place their trust in Him again.

The song breaks into a beautiful refrain of God's presence in verse four. It sings of a river whose streams shall make glad the city of God; whose waters reach into the holy place of the tabernacles of the Most High. God is in the midst of her, His city, where His presence dwells. The people of God can rest and take their joy in this fact: their El Elyon (the Most High God) is with them. And it's here in the knowledge of His presence that a bright and fresh assurance is given for future distress, "God shall help her and that right early." He has proven to be a very present help in the past and He promises to help her the moment she acknowledges Him. He is at hand to protect, preserve and provide.

In verse six, the song gives a reminder of God's past dealings with enemy nations. With a mere utterance of His voice, He was able to remove kingdoms and melt the earth. Surely their Elohim, who brought the existence of heaven and earth into being by the power of His Word, who had displayed His mighty power on their behalf by removing enemy nations, was able to use His power to protect them today. The Lord of hosts was with them! He is the commander and chief of the armies of heaven. If God is for them who could stand against them? He makes wars to cease unto the ends of the earth. He can disarm and disable all that would try to rise up against His people.

The song then issues a command from God, "Be still and know that I am God." God is saying: *Remember My past help and recognize My presence with you today. Let this knowledge help you to let go of your fears. And if your faith is still wavering then consider this: I have determined that I will be exalted. This is a promise and I cannot lie. I will perform what I have proclaimed. You are my chosen and precious possession, you bear my name and I have made a covenant to protect and provide for you. For my name sake I will be honored and glorified.*

Psalm 138:2 says, "I bow before Your holy temple as I worship. I praise Your name for Your unfailing love and faithfulness: for Your promises are backed by all the honor of Your name" (NLT).

If, after considering His past faithfulness and present promise of help your heart is still unsettled, let this settle it: God will be exalted! You can count on it!

Let us pick up this pattern that God has laid down in Psalm 46 to RECOGNIZE, REMEMBER, RECEIVE and REST. In this study we will be growing in the knowledge of God's character and attributes, remembering His presence, power and provision, receiving His promises, and finding rest for our souls.

Begin by reading through Psalm 46.

1. Record your thoughts.

2. What commands are given in this Psalm?

3. In verse 10 we are commanded to "Be still and know that I am God." Look up the words "to know" in the concordance and write out the definition.

We are able to understand from this definition that we are to be actively engaged in learning and finding out about God. We should be able to distinguish, discern and recognize His character, ability, plans, promises and purposes. We are to be skillful, wise and well-acquainted with His Word. It also speaks of knowing God by experience. It is crucial for us to exercise our faith in order to know Him intimately. We have a history with God!

4. Read through Psalm 46 again and record what you recognize and learn about God.

5. In what ways does this knowledge help you to let go of the things that are trying to disturb your peace today?

We are also commanded to "behold His works" (verse 8). There is a strengthening of our faith that is produced as we recognize and remember the ability of God. This faith is just what we need when fear tries to creep in and take hold of us! Our hearts can easily get overwhelmed when we forget about God's blessings, benefits, power and presence.

6. As you read through Psalm 46, record what you behold about the works of God, His power, presence and provision.

7. Read Psalm 63. What things did David remember about God and what did that stir up in him?

The promises of God give us hope of a future good. Reading about God's promises is not enough to calm our fears about the future, by faith we must trust that God will perform what He has promised to do.

8. What promises are given in Psalm 46?

9. As you meditate upon the knowledge of God, the works of God, and the promises of God, what is stirred up in you?

Recognize

Growing in the knowledge of His character and ability. What did you learn about God; His ability, plans, and purposes?

Remember

Recalling His blessings and benefits that you have experienced.

Receive

Has God reassured you with a promise this week?

Rest

In light of all you learned about God's character, ability, and promises, what are you able to release to His faithful care?

CHAPTER

2

KNOW YOUR GOD

God is our refuge and strength, a very present help in trouble. Therefore we will not fear, even though the earth be removed, and though the mountains be carried into the midst of the sea; though its waters roar and be troubled, though the mountains shake with its swelling.
Psalm 46:1-3

Psalm 46 begins with the powerful proclamation, "God is our refuge and strength, a very present help in trouble." He is a refuge, the One to whom we can flee and hide when danger comes. God, Himself, is a shelter, a place of safety for us when we feel threatened or fearful, when we need rest. He is also a strength, our strength. We all have moments, even seasons, when we are weak, feeling vulnerable, discouraged or weary. God is our strength, the One who possesses unlimited power to protect and preserve.

1. Read the following Psalms and record what you learn about God as your refuge and source of strength.

Psalm 61

Psalm 62:5-8

Psalm 91:1-11

Our lives seem to be in no lack of trouble. In Job 5:7 it says, "Man is born to trouble, as sure as the sparks fly upward." And Jesus told His disciples, "In this world you will have trouble." He followed up with this faith fortifying statement, "But be of good courage, I have overcome the world" (John 16:33). Take heart, friend, Jesus has already conquered all that had power to ultimately destroy you! We are more than conquerors in Christ because the territory of our lives has been won and a portion of the spoils is peace and joy in Jesus Christ! We will have trouble, adversity, affliction and tribulation. We may even experience times of distress and anguish. But be of good courage! These are temporary and momentary and "are achieving for us an eternal glory that far outweighs them all" (2 Corinthians 4:17, NIV).

God is a very present help in trouble. He is a constant, great and abundant force to be found and proven sufficient to help. The wholeness of God is present to help. He doesn't divide His power, presence or attention, but is fully present in His muchness and totality to protect and preserve you. Isn't it a great comfort to know that God doesn't get distracted and never shows up unprepared or preoccupied. The fullness of His power is always at hand to help, support and aid you.

"Because You have been my help, therefore in the shadow of your wings will I rejoice." Psalm 63:7

"God is our refuge and strength, a very present help in trouble. Therefore we will not fear, even though the earth be removed, and though the mountains be carried into the midst of the sea; though its waters roar and be troubled, though the mountains shake with its swelling" (Psalm 46:1–3). That is a lot of "thoughs."

Even *though* every earthly comfort and support be removed
and *though* things are falling apart around me
though there is trouble surrounding me
and *though* the ground under my feet is unstable

I will choose not to fear because I know God is my hiding place. He is my strength, my Rock. He is my very present help in my time of trouble.

2. Write out verses one and two from Psalm 46, personalizing them.

Hagar was a woman who was blessed to have known God by experience. Her first amazing encounter with Him actually changed the way she perceived God and gave her strength to face her trouble.

Read Genesis 16 and record your first thoughts:

3. What do you learn about God from verses 7 and 8?

**4. God responds to Hagar with instruction, a
   promise and a prophecy. Record each one.**

   Verse 9 (Instruction):

   Verse 10 (Promise):

   Verses 11 and 12 (Prophecy):

5. What was Hagar's response in verse 13?

6. How do you think this personal experience with God gave Hagar the courage and strength to return to her trouble?

7. It is one thing to return to a difficult situation and quite another to yield yourself to it! Why do you think Hagar was able to submit herself to Sarai?

8. Is there someone or something you are avoiding or running away from?

9. How does knowing that God sees you encourage you to face your trouble?

10. God also instructed Hagar to name her son Ishmael.

What is the meaning of this name?

In what ways do you think this became a future source of encouragement to Hagar?

11. How does the knowledge that God hears you in your distress help you to be still?

God saw and heard Hagar in her distress. He sought her out and became her very present help in her time of trouble. He put courage into her with His presence, by His concern and through His promise. God didn't change Hagar's circumstances, but her encounter with God must have changed her, because thereafter she called Him by a new name, El Roi. The New Living Translation reads, "Thereafter, Hagar used another name to refer to the LORD, who had spoken to her. She said, 'You are the God who sees me.' She also said 'Have I truly seen the One who sees me?'" (Genesis 16:13)

12. When you think back to your history with God can you think of a THEREAFTER time when God revealed Himself to you personally and it forever changed the way you perceive Him?

God's presence, prophecy and promise brought comfort to Hagar. He put strength into her and made her brave to return to a difficult circumstance.

13. Read 2 Corinthians 1:3-5.

What do you learn about God?

Research the word *COMFORT* from these verses.

What do you learn about the comfort of God?

What does God's comfort produce in His children?

May your heart be quieted by the presence and power of God. He is your refuge, strength and very present help. He sees you, He hears you and He knows you.

Recognize

Growing in the knowledge of His character and ability. What did you learn about God; His ability, plans, and purposes?

Remember

Recalling His blessings and benefits that you have experienced.

Receive

Has God reassured you with a promise this week?

Rest

In light of all you learned about God's character, ability, and promises, what are you able to release to His faithful care?

CHAPTER
3

KNOW GOD'S CHARACTER

There is a river whose streams shall make glad the city of God,
the holy place of the tabernacle of the Most High.
God is in the midst of her, she shall not be moved; God shall help her,
just at the break of dawn.
Psalm 46:4-5

Stillness. Our hearts and minds long for it. We want to let go of worrying, to refrain from fretting, to be quiet and rest. Our Heavenly Father is good. Like any good parent, His desire is for His children to rest in the assurance that He is able to care for them. He wants us to be free from fear, anxiety and dread of the future. Our faith must be engaged and activated if we are to remain at peace. Second Corinthians 10:3–5 says, "For though we walk in the flesh, we do not war according to the flesh. For the weapons of our warfare are not carnal but mighty in God for pulling down strongholds, casting down arguments and every high thing that exalts itself against the knowledge of God, bringing every thought into captivity to the obedience of Christ."

The most powerful weapons we possess for combating fear are knowledge of and faith in God! And it is knowledge and faith in God that must be exalted if we are to conquer doubt. The writer of Psalm 46 paints a worst-case scenario in verses 2 and 3.

Even though the earth be removed,
and though the mountains be carried away into
the midst of the sea, though its waters roar and be
troubled, though the mountains shake with its swelling ...

He sets this dramatic picture right up against the knowledge of who God is; God is a refuge and strength, a very present help in trouble. He exalts the character of God against calamity and can proclaim, "We will not fear." Even if we are surrounded with instability, chaos, and trouble; even when all earthly help and support have been removed, God is with us. Though the pressures of life and the concerns of the future try to overwhelm us, we have this knowledge: God is present. He is with us and He is for us. Not only is He our hiding place, our strength and our very present help in times of trouble, He is also an overflowing force of faithful goodness coming towards us.

There is a river whose streams shall make glad the city
of God, the holy place of the tabernacle of the Most High.
God is in the midst of her, she shall not be moved.
God shall help her, just at the break of dawn.
Psalm 46:4–5

Jerusalem was God's chosen city, the place of worship and meeting with Him. God manifested His presence and His glory in the Temple. It was in the midst of that place that right relationship with God was restored and communion was maintained. God's goodness dwelt with His people. Be still and know that I am good! This is a substantial truth about the character of God that we can plant the feet of our faith upon and stand with firmness!

1. **Choose to look into as much of the goodness of God as you desire and record what you discover.**

   Nahum 1:7

   Psalm 31:19–20

   Psalm 84:11

   Psalm 100:5

   Nehemiah 9:20

And the LORD passed by before him, and proclaimed,
"The LORD, the LORD God, merciful and gracious,
longsuffering, and abundant in goodness and truth."
Exodus 34:6

God is a strong force of abounding goodness. All the facets of His goodness stream to us through the indwelling presence of the Holy Spirit.

There is a river whose streams make glad the city of God.

His goodness streams in HOPE. When disappointment tries to muddy our view of the future, recognizing His goodness has the power to restore a right perspective.

Read Romans 15:13.

2. What do you recognize about the character of God?

3. What is God able to do?

4. What is your part?

Read Jeremiah 29:10–11.

5. What are you able to discern about the character of God from these verses?

His goodness streams in MERCY. We are always in need of new mercies from God. And His goodness ensures that His mercy continues to flow to us.

6. Read the following verses and record what you discover.

Psalm 25:6–7

Psalm 107:1–9

His goodness streams in FAITH. Our faith can wither and fail in the face of adversity. God's goodness streams in and refreshes our faith and brings a fresh courage to our countenance.

7. Read Psalm 27:13–14. Record your thoughts.

His goodness streams in PEACE and JOY. God's presence reaches into the depths of our being in such a way that even in the worst of circumstances peace and joy flow and bubble up.

8. Let these truths overflow you!

Isaiah 54:10

Isaiah 55:11–13

Psalm 105:37–45

What threatens your peace and joy today? Will you stop and take some time to recognize the goodness of your God, remember His mercies, receive His kindness, and rest in His faithfulness?

9. Let the goodness of God restore and refresh
your soul. Choose a name or attribute of God
to research and record what you discover.

10. Write out a prayer that acknowledges who He is in the midst of your concerns and cares.

You keep him in perfect peace whose mind is stayed on you, because he trusts in you.
Isaiah 26:3

Recognize

Growing in the knowledge of His character and ability. What did you learn about God; His ability, plans, and purposes?

Remember

Recalling His blessings and benefits that you have experienced.

Receive

Has God reassured you with a promise this week?

Rest

In light of all you learned about God's character, ability, and promises, what are you able to release to His faithful care?

CHAPTER
4

KNOW GOD'S ABILITY

The nations raged, the kingdoms were moved; He uttered His voice, the earth melted.
The LORD of hosts is with us; the God of Jacob is our refuge. Selah
Come, behold the works of the LORD, Who has made desolations in the earth.
He makes wars cease to the end of the earth; He breaks the bow and cuts the spear
in two; He burns the chariot in the fire.
Psalm 46:6-9

Remembering the wonderful work God has done and recalling the power of His faithful aid in times past is like a strong shield and sword for our faith today. Recounting His past blessings and benefits surrounds us like a shield and protects us with a confidence in His present ability to help. Recalling what He is capable of accomplishing is like a sword in hand—it is powerful to help advance us in our present challenges.

"The LORD of hosts is with us"(!!!) the song bursts out in verse seven. The commander and chief of the armies of heaven is present with us! Now that is a powerful proclamation that gets our attention. "The God of Jacob is our refuge. Selah." The God of the past is the same yesterday, today and forever. He was the hiding place for Abraham, Isaac, Jacob, David, John, and Paul, and He is our refuge today. Selah … rest and pause there. As you let your heart and mind sink into the weightiness of that truth it is then prepared to "behold the works of the LORD."

David was a man whose life was filled with trouble, danger, threats, betrayal, and loss. When he felt the pressures of life heavy laden upon his soul he ran to his proven refuge and strength. God was his very present help. David took time to remember and behold the works of his God. His habit was to remember God's past faithfulness and help. He looked at His God in the midst of trouble and recounted His many benefits and blessings. This would open up a fresh stream of hope and faith that supplied David with a stillness of soul. Psalm 103 is an excellent example of David beholding the works of the LORD. As he meditated upon all that God had done and was capable of doing, the presence of God became a source of adoration and celebration.

> *Bless the LORD, O my soul;*
> *And all that is within me, bless His holy name!*
> *Bless the LORD, O my soul,*
> *And forget not all His benefits:*
> *Who forgives all your iniquities,*
> *Who heals all your diseases,*
> *Who redeems your life from destruction,*
> *Who crowns you with lovingkindness and tender mercies,*
> *Who satisfies your mouth with good things,*
> *So that your youth is renewed like the eagle's.*
> *The LORD executes righteousness*
> *And justice for all who are oppressed.*
> *He made known His ways to Moses,*

His acts to the children of Israel.
The LORD is merciful and gracious,
Slow to anger, and abounding in mercy.
He will not always strive with us,
Nor will He keep His anger forever.
He has not dealt with us according to our sins,
Nor punished us according to our iniquities.
For as the heavens are high above the earth,
So great is His mercy toward those who fear Him;
As far as the east is from the west,
So far has He removed our transgressions from us.
As a father pities his children,
So the LORD pities those who fear Him.
For He knows our frame;
He remembers that we are dust.
As for man, his days are like grass;
As a flower of the field, so he flourishes.
For the wind passes over it, and it is gone,
And its place remembers it no more.
But the mercy of the LORD is from everlasting to everlasting
On those who fear Him,
And His righteousness to children's children,
To such as keep His covenant,
And to those who remember His commandments to do them.
The LORD has established His throne in heaven,
And His kingdom rules over all.
Bless the LORD, you His angels,
Who excel in strength, who do His word,
Heeding the voice of His word.
Bless the LORD, all you His hosts,
You ministers of His, who do His pleasure.
Bless the LORD, all His works,
In all places of His dominion.
Bless the LORD, O my soul!

"Bless the Lord" means to kneel down; adore and celebrate Him. A sure way to quiet an anxious heart is by humbling it before God, beholding His character and ability, adoring Him for His care and celebrating His power.

1. Read through Psalm 103 and take note of the following:

In what ways do you notice David expressing humility?

What did David behold about the character of God?

What did David behold about the abilities of God?

What did David adore about God?

In what ways do you sense David stirring up a celebration of God?

2. Thoughtfully read through Psalm 57. See if you are able to recognize David's response to trouble.

   Describe how you perceive David bowing himself before the LORD.

   What does David recall and remember about God?

   What does David adore about God?

   How does David stir up a celebrating of God?

3. What is disturbing your peace and joy today?

4. Read the following verses and record the benefits of bowing before God in times of trouble.

Psalm 18:27

Psalm 149:4

Isaiah 57:15

James 4:10

5. Read 1 Peter 5:6–9 and record your thoughts.

6. What do you need to behold about the ability of God that will help you to rest quietly in Him?

7. What blessings and benefits have you received from God recently?

8. How does recounting these blessings strengthen your faith in light of your current difficulties?

9. Can you recall a time from your past when God came to your aid?

It is easy to lose sight of God's blessings and benefits when a storm comes rolling in. His past faithfulness sometimes is obscured by the dark clouds of today's trouble. A sure way to blow away those clouds of doubt is to purposefully remember His benefits. David proclaimed, "forget not all His benefits." In Psalm 56:2–4 he declared, "My foes have trampled upon me all day long, For they are many who fight proudly against me. When I am afraid, I will put my trust in You. In God, whose word I praise, In God I have put my trust; I shall not be afraid. What can mere man do to me?" (NASB) Do you ever feel as though the enemy of your faith has been trampling upon you all day long? This is the time to remember your God, the champion of your faith, and recall His many blessings and benefits.

Write out a prayer to God in adoration and celebration of all He has done for you.

Recognize

Growing in the knowledge of His character and ability. What did you learn about God; His ability, plans, and purposes?

Remember

Recalling His blessings and benefits that you have experienced.

Receive

Has God reassured you with a promise this week?

Rest

In light of all you learned about God's character, ability, and promises, what are you able to release to His faithful care?

CHAPTER
5

KNOW GOD'S PROMISES

*Be still, and know that I am God; I will be exalted among the nations,
I will be exalted in the earth!*
Psalm 46:10

To simply be told to "be still" can often cause anxiety all in itself! We hear it, know it, and we want it, but we are sometimes bewildered by the command. The most powerful truth we have to help keep our minds at peace is actually found right in verse ten of Psalm 46, but for some reason it is often left out of our reciting and we are left wondering: *How? How can I be still in this circumstance?* The "how" is always found in the "Who." Look again at the entirety of verse ten. What follows the command from God to "be still" is a promise from Him that He will be exalted among the nations and upon the earth. Here, in this potent promise, is the firm foundation upon which we can stand steadily, release our fears and let go of our worries. God has determined He will be exalted. It is a promise upon which our faith may safely rest. It is a promise that is higher than us and much higher than our present trouble. We sometimes get so overwhelmed by our current difficulty that we can lose our spiritual perspective. We may forget that "My thoughts are not your thoughts, nor are your ways My ways," says the LORD. "For as the heavens are higher than the earth, so are My ways higher than your ways and my thoughts than your thoughts" (Isaiah 55:8–9). God will get His glory from our lives. He just might not be accomplishing that work in a way we understand. But we can be sure of His presence and help while He completes the good work He has begun. We have His promise and pledge that He will be exalted. This is the answer to the "how" we can be still. It is the "Who" that has made a promise to uphold the honor of His name. We can trust and receive a promise when we have confidence in the integrity and power of the promise giver. Our hearts can be still because we know and believe in the One who promises. We know His character and His ability, therefore, we can sink down into His faithful word.

   1. **Read the following verses and record what you learn about the integrity and power of our God.**

   I can be still because I know that God is faithful ...

   Deuteronomy 7:9

   Isaiah 14:24

Isaiah 54:10

I can be still because I know that God is all-powerful ...

Genesis 18:14

Isaiah 14:27

Isaiah 43:13

Matthew 19:26

I can be still because I know that God is immutable ...

Malachi 3:6

James 1:17

I can be still because I know that God cannot lie ...

Numbers 23:19

Titus 1:2

Hebrews 6:13–20

God is building in us a faith in Him that is unshakable. This is what pleases Him and how He receives the greatest glory from our lives. Abraham is a man that we often associate with great faith. But Abraham started out just like the rest of us. God gave him a mustard seed of faith and a promise, and Abraham had to flick that seed into the ground of God's Word. When Abraham would honor God by planting a seed of faith, God would honor Abraham by giving him more faith. And so it went, until Abraham had so much faith in God and His promises that he didn't waver no matter how impossible the promises appeared.

¹⁶ Therefore it is of faith that it might be according to grace, so that the promise might be sure to all the seed, not only to those who are of the law, but also to those who are of the faith of Abraham, who is the father of us all ¹⁷ (as it is written, "I have made you a father of many nations") in the presence of Him whom he believed—God, who gives life to the dead and calls those things which do not exist as though they did; ¹⁸ who, contrary to hope, in hope believed, so that he became the father of many nations, according to what was spoken, "So shall your descendants be." ¹⁹ And not being weak in faith, he did not consider his own body, already dead (since he was about a hundred years old), and the deadness of Sarah's womb. ²⁰ He did not waver at the promise of God through unbelief, but was strengthened in faith, giving glory to God, ²¹ and being fully convinced that what He had promised He was also able to perform.

Romans 4:16–21

2. According to Romans 4:19 and 20, what things did Abraham *not* do?

"Not being weak in faith" does not necessarily mean that Abraham's faith was strong, but literally means that he used what faith he had. He didn't abstain from using whatever strength of faith he possessed. Abraham did not consider the deadness of his own body or the deadness of Sarah's womb. This means that he didn't observe or fix his attention upon the impossibility of what God had promised. Instead, he considered the One who made the promise. Abraham revered God's Word more than He respected the deadness of his and Sarah's bodies. He beheld his God and fixed his eyes on the Author and Perfecter of his faith. Abraham also did not waver at the promise of God through unbelief. In Matthew Henry's commentary on Romans 4:16–21 he says, "Unbelief is at the bottom of all our staggerings at God's promises. The strength of faith appeared in its victory over fears. God honors faith and great faith honors God." Twenty-five years had passed from the time God gave Abraham the promise of a child until he and Sarah received Isaac. There were probably many times over those years that Abraham had to toss in his seeds of faith, and every time God rewarded him with a strengthening of his faith.

3. **What can you learn and apply to your life from what Abraham did *not* do with God's promises?**

4. **What did Abraham do according to Romans 4:16–21?**

5. **Explain verse 18a ("Who, contrary to hope, in hope believed") in your own words.**

6. What do you learn about God's character from this portion of Scripture?

7. What do you discover about the ability of God?

8. What do you perceive about the promises of God?

9. Is there something in your life right now you have considered dead? Fix your eyes on God and cast your seeds of faith on His promises. Write out a prayer expressing your need for a fortifying of your faith.

I can be still because all of God's promises have been fulfilled in Christ Jesus. Abraham had God's Word in which to place his trust. We have God's Word, the testimony of Jesus Christ's death and resurrection, and the indwelling of the Holy Spirit in our hearts witnessing and confirming the guarantee of God's promises.

> *For Jesus Christ, the Son of God, does not waver between "Yes" and "No." He is the one whom Silas, Timothy, and I preached to you, and as God's ultimate "Yes," he always does what he says. For all of God's promises have been fulfilled in Christ with a resounding "Yes!" And through Christ, our "Amen" (which means "Yes") ascends to God for his glory. It is God who enables us, along with you, to stand firm for Christ. He has commissioned us, and he has identified us as his own by placing the Holy Spirit in our hearts as the first installment that guarantees everything he has promised to us.*
>
> 2 Corinthians 1:19–22 (NLT)

Through these verses in 2 Corinthians we can see the trinity working together to confirm all of God's promises. The promises are made by the God of truth who cannot lie. They are made in Jesus Christ who is the Amen, the True and Faithful witness who has purchased and validated the covenant of promises with His blood. Jesus is the surety of the covenant (Hebrews 7:22). The promises are confirmed by the Holy Spirit. The Holy Spirit confirms and establishes Christians in the faith of the gospel. He is given as an earnest in our hearts. An earnest secures the promises so we are able—by faith in the blood of Christ—to say, "Amen!" to all the promises of God. We glorify God by believing His Word.

10. Take some time to research the word "amen" from 2 Corinthians 1:20. Record what you discover.

The word "amen" is a most remarkable word. It was transliterated directly from the Hebrew into the Greek of the New Testament, then into Latin and into English and many other languages, so that it is practically a universal word. It has been called the best known word in human speech. The word is directly related—in fact, almost identical— to the Hebrew word for "believe" (amam), or faithful. Thus, it came to mean "sure" or "truly," an expression of absolute trust and confidence."

Blueletterbible.com

Those who place their faith in God's promises receive peace and joy even in the midst of trouble. When we say "amen" to a promise from God we bring our minds into agreement with Him. When our thoughts line up with His thoughts they are brought under His authority and His shalom is established within. A faithful "sure" to God and His promises brings a solid peace to our souls. We stagger at God's promises when we doubt God's character, power, and presence.

As we declare, "Amen, I believe you, Lord," it ushers in joy that permeates beyond the surface of our lives and penetrates to the core of our being. The joy of the Lord is the strength of our faith during difficult times because it fortifies our inner man. Fear and worry exhaust our faith. Receiving God's promises by faith brings a joy that keeps us standing firm in the most trying of times.

Our hearts can be still as we actively agree with God and place our trust in His faithful, unchanging, true, good, and capable hands. We honor God by giving Him our faith and receiving His promises with a resounding "Amen!" He, in return, honors us with even more faith, peace, and joy.

> For example, there was God's promise to Abraham. Since there was no one greater to swear by, God took an oath in his own name, saying: "I will certainly bless you, and I will multiply your descendants beyond number." Then Abraham waited patiently, and he received what God had promised. Now when people take an oath, they call on someone greater than themselves to hold them to it. And without any question that oath is binding. God also bound himself with an oath, so that those who received the promise could be perfectly sure that he would never change his mind. So God has given both his promise and his oath. These two things are unchangeable because it is impossible for God to lie. Therefore, we who have fled to him for refuge can have great confidence as we hold to the hope that lies before us. This hope is a strong and trustworthy anchor for our souls. It leads us through the curtain into God's inner sanctuary. Jesus has already gone in there for us. He has become our eternal High Priest in the order of Melchizedek.
>
> Hebrews 6:13–20 (NLT)

11. Is your soul staggering in the midst of a present difficulty? Will you search out the promises of God and find one that you can respond to with a resounding "AMEN." This hope in His promise will be like an anchor to your soul keeping you from being tossed around and drowning in doubt. Write out your promise personalizing it. May God honor you with a strengthening of your faith. May He refresh you with joy, and settle you in His peace. May He be glorified in your life today.

Recognize

Growing in the knowledge of His character and ability. What did you learn about God; His ability, plans, and purposes?

Remember

Recalling His blessings and benefits that you have experienced.

Receive

Has God reassured you with a promise this week?

Rest

In light of all you learned about God's character, ability, and promises, what are you able to release to His faithful care?

CHAPTER
6
KNOW GOD IS WITH YOU

The LORD of hosts is with us.
Psalm 46:11a

Be still. This is a command issued from a good and faithful Heavenly Father spoken with loving authority over each of His children's lives. Let's take a look at what God is communicating with this command.

1. **Research "be still" from Psalm 46:10 in your concordance. Record what you discover.**

2. Is there anything new or surprising to you about the definition of "be still"?

3. Rewrite verse 10a in your own words. (Rewrite it as many times and ways as you are inspired!)

"Be still and know that the LORD of hosts is with us." This is our greatest assurance and reason for remaining at rest. The knowledge and awareness of His presence brings an immediate strengthening to whatever might be weak within us. In the previous chapters we have looked at the value of recognizing and remembering the character and capability of God to help keep our souls quiet. We have also looked at the necessity of receiving His promises for our future so that we can maintain a calm confidence in Him when our futures look uncertain. It is good to look both backward and forward and see that God is there for us. But often times it is in the now that we can lose sight of His very present presence. God with us *now* is at the heart of Psalm 46:

He is a very present help ...

God is in the midst of her, she shall not be moved.

The LORD of hosts is with us.

All of creation has an omnipresent God in its midst, "'Can anyone hide from me in a secret place? Am I not everywhere in all the heavens and earth?' says the LORD" (Jeremiah 23:24, NLT). The Jews were a chosen people with special favor from God. The Bible records many holy visitations from God with His people (Abraham in Genesis 18, Moses in Exodus 6:6 and 33:11, Joshua in Joshua 5:13, Jacob in Genesis 28:16 and 32:22–32, just to note a few). God's presence was with His people in a cloud by day and a fire by night as He led His children through the wilderness to the promise land. God also manifested His presence with them in the Tabernacle and Temple where they would go to meet with Him.

What a tremendous privilege we have been given today as the children of God's grace. We have no need to visit a building or offer an animal sacrifice to gain access to God. We simply place our faith in the spotless Lamb of God as the substitutionary sacrifice for our sins and we are granted access to God and given the indwelling presence of His Holy Spirit into our hearts. By placing our faith in Jesus' death, burial, and resurrection, we are saved from the wrath of God to come. We are delivered from the power of darkness, transferred into the kingdom of light, and given eternal life with a place and an inheritance waiting for us in heaven.

God is in the midst of us and we shall not be moved. His Holy Spirit has been given to help us, empower us, enable us, guide us, comfort us, teach us, and to manifest the reality of His presence with us now. We are the temple of the living God. We are earthen vessels made immortal carrying around with us Immortality everywhere we go! We have been given His Holy Spirit as a seal. We are marked by the Spirit as belonging to God. There is no power on earth or in heaven that can separate us from His presence. It is also comforting to know that we received His Holy Spirit by grace, and His Spirit remains in us by grace. We never earned or merited the favor of His indwelling presence. This means our mistakes, failures and backsliding cannot remove His presence from us. What a great confidence we can have in our Constant Companion. He promises to never leave us or forsake us, and we know He cannot lie and will never change His mind. He is happy to be stuck with us!

The awareness of the nearness of God is a calming comfort that can settle the most troubled heart. To simply know God is with us is like a soothing hush whispered over our souls and we are quieted deep within.

4. **Read the following verses and write
them out personalizing each one.**

1 Corinthians 3:16

Deuteronomy 31:6

Isaiah 43:1–5

Matthew 28:20

Psalm 46:1, 5, 7

**5. As your awareness of His presence with you *now*
is heightened through the reading of the previous
verses what is produced in your heart and mind?**

A.W. Tozer wrote in his book, *God's Pursuit of Man,* "We
habitually stand in our now and look back in faith to see our past
filled with God. We look forward and see Him inhabiting our future;
but our now is uninhabited except for ourselves. Thus we are
guilty of a kind of temporary atheism which leaves us alone in the
universe, while for a time, God is not."

The presence of God's Spirit dwelling in us is the most glorious
gift God has given us while here on earth! But too often we fail to
acknowledge He is with us *now.* When we do this our souls stagger
at the difficulties of life. When we feel the outside pressures of life
pressing in upon us we must recognize and remember Who is on
the inside able to exert a greater force to still, strengthen, and help.
His presence calms us down and cheers us up!

Practicing God's presence is part of the pattern for maintaining
a peaceful and joyful life with God. With God's help we can cultivate
a habit of awareness of His nearness.

The following excerpt is taken from a book titled, *The Practice of the Presence of God,* written by Brother Lawrence (it is written in the third person).

> *For the past forty years his continual care has been to be always with God; and to do nothing, say nothing, and think nothing which may displease Him. He does this without any view or motive except pure love of Him and because God deserves infinitely more.*
>
> *He is now so accustomed to that Divine presence that he receives from it continual comfort and peace. For about thirty years his soul has been filled with joy and delight so continual, and sometimes so great, that he is forced to find ways to hide their appearing outwardly to others who may not understand.*
>
> *If sometimes he becomes a little distracted from that Divine presence, God gently recalls Himself by a stirring in his soul. This often happens when he is most engaged in his outward chores and tasks. He answers with exact fidelity to these inward drawings, either by an elevation of his heart towards God, or by a meek and fond regard to Him, or by such words as love forms upon these occasions. For instance, he may say, "My God, here I am all devoted to You," or "Lord, make me according to Your heart."*

It seems to him (in fact, he feels it) that this God of love, satisfied with such few words, reposes again and rests in the depth and center of his soul. The experience of these things gives him such certainty that God is always in the innermost part of his soul that he is beyond doubting it under any circumstances.

Brother Lawrence lived in France during the 17th century. He became known for his simple and humble way of worship. He was a monk assigned to the monastery kitchen where he was given the tedious chores of cooking and cleaning under the authority and demands of his superiors. He experienced the value of maintaining an awareness of God's presence in everyday work. In his Maxims, Lawrence writes, "Men invent means and methods of coming at God's love, they learn rules and set up devices to remind them of that love, and it seems like a world of trouble to bring oneself into the consciousness of God's presence. Yet it might be so simple. Is it not quicker and easier just to do our common business wholly for the love of him?"

6. What inspires you from what is quoted here from Brother Lawrence?

7. What tends to hinder your awareness of the presence of God?

I have set the LORD continually before me;
because He is at my right hand, I will not be shaken.
Therefore my heart is glad and my glory rejoices;
my flesh also will dwell securely.
Psalm 16:8–9 (NLT)

8. What can you do to cultivate an awareness of God's presence continually?

Write out a prayer to God asking Him to help keep you aware of His presence at all times.

9. As you acknowledge the presence of God with you now, finish the following sentences:

I can let go of …

I can cease from …

I will refrain from …

I can be still because …

Recognize

Growing in the knowledge of His character and ability. What did you learn about God; His ability, plans, and purposes?

Remember

Recalling His blessings and benefits that you have experienced.

Receive

Has God reassured you with a promise this week?

Rest

In light of all you learned about God's character, ability, and promises, what are you able to release to His faithful care?

CHAPTER
7

KNOW YOU ARE IN HIM

The God of Jacob is our refuge.
Psalm 46:11b

We can simply be in Christ by faith and rest in our Almighty Refuge. This is possibly our most comforting and challenging call from God. He is telling us, "*Be* who you already are by faith." You are in Him, His word, His promises, and His presence. We came to Him empty, desperate, alone, and dependent; with nothing and needing everything. And He continues to bring us back to these blessed truths: we are His children, He is our Father; apart from Him we can do nothing and are nothing. With Him all things are possible. His everlasting invitation to us is:

Come to me all you who are weary and heavy burdened and I will give you rest ... unto your souls.

Cast all your cares upon Me for I care for you.

The Lord will perfect those things that concern you.

We can "trust in Him at all times, pour out our hearts before Him because He is a refuge for us."

We have looked into Psalm forty-six to discover a pattern we can follow to keep our hearts at rest. God exhorts His children to rest in the knowledge of His present help. He was the Israelite's strength and power, their watchman who kept them, protected them, and provided for them. Because they had past experience with His faithfulness they knew Him to be a refuge in Whom they could run and hide. He was in the very midst of His people and they had a safe place in Him. In the shelter of His wing they could let go of their fears and find rest. God is with us even in the darkest of valleys. He is able to deliver us from the deepest pits and will rescue us when we are utterly cast down. There is no trouble we will meet that will be faced alone. God is always at hand to help. He is in us. He surrounds us. He is beyond us and behind us. He is upon us and He is for us. In our Refuge we can be weak, be feeble, be still, and be quiet. Our fretting, fixing, and fearing only serve to keep us from His Almighty care. We must come to an end of self-effort and come to God as a helpless child. "God must be everything for us, our part is to yield and rest" (A.W. Tozer).

God's almighty omnipotence is always at work with our trust. We are to BE and He DOES. We are kept by the power of God through faith.

He who dwells in the secret place of the Most High
shall abide under the shadow of the Almighty.
I will say of the LORD, "He is my refuge and my fortress;
my God, in Him I will trust."
surely He shall deliver you from the snare of the fowler
and from the perilous pestilence.
He shall cover you with His feathers,
and under His wings you shall take refuge.
Psalm 91:1–4

1. What are the names of God used in Psalm 91:1–4?

What are the meanings of these names?

2. According to these verses what does God provide in Himself for His children?

3. What is our part in receiving these benefits?

Keep me as the apple of Your eye;
hide me under the shadow of Your wings.
Psalm 17:8

The word "keep" in this verse means to guard, protect, keep watch, save life, have charge over, to keep within bounds, restrain, preserve, and reserve.

4. Read 1 Peter 1:3–5.

What is reserved and preserved for us by our Keeper?

How are these things protected?

What is our part?

5. The word "hide" from Psalm 17:8 means to conceal and carefully hide. Read the following verses and note what you learn about God being your hiding place.

Psalm 27:5

Psalm 31:2

Isaiah 49:1–2

6. God hides us under the shadow of His wings. Read the following verses and record what you learn about the shadow of God.

Psalm 57:1

Psalm 63:7

Hosea 14:7

Isaiah 4:6

7. Read Psalm 121. Record what you learn about your Keeper and His promises to care for you.

We are kept by the power of our Almighty God through faith. He is our refuge, our fortress, our strong tower, our shade, our strength, and salvation. He hides us in His secret pavilion, under the shadow of His wings. His feathers spread over us and we are hidden in the hollow of His hand. We have a safe place in God to let go and rest.

> *The great hindrance to trust is self effort. As long as you have your own wisdom and thoughts and strength, you cannot fully trust God. But when God breaks you down, when everything begins to grow dim before your eyes and you see that you understand nothing, then God is near. If you will wait upon God, He will become all you need. As long as we are something, God cannot be all, and His omnipotence cannot do its full work. That is the beginning of faith— utter despair of self and dependence on God alone.*
> Andrew Murray, *Absolute Surrender.*

In Matthew 5, Jesus described the condition of people who are truly blessed.

**8. Read Matthew 5:3–11 and use your own words
to describe who Jesus says is blessed.**

9. Why are you blessed when …

   You are poor in spirit?

You are mournful over sin or loss?

You are meek?

You are hungry and thirsty for a right standing with God?

You are merciful?

You are pure in heart?

10. Research the word "meek" (Matthew 5:5) in a concordance and record the definition.

Meekness toward God is that disposition of spirit in which we accept His dealings with us as good, and therefore without disputing or resisting. In the OT, the meek are those wholly relying on God rather than their own strength to defend against injustice. Thus, meekness toward evil people means knowing God is permitting the injuries they inflict, that He is using them to purify His elect, and that He will deliver His elect in His time (Isa. 41:17, Luke 18:1–8). Gentleness or meekness is the opposite of self-assertiveness and self-interest. It stems from trust in God's goodness and control over the situation. The gentle person is not occupied with self at all. This is a work of the Holy Spirit, not of the human will (Gal. 5:23).

Outline of Biblical Usage, Blueletterbible.com

11. What importance does the quality of meekness have for one who desires to be still?

We can release our cares and burdens as we rest in the knowledge of His character. We must actively learn more about His attributes and exercise our faith so we have personal experience with Him. Then when trouble comes we can quickly recognize Him, acknowledge who He is, and our hearts will have good reason to remain calm.

We can cease from striving and self-effort when we take time to remember the wonderful works of our LORD. Our daily pattern for living by faith is strengthened when we recall His past faithfulness and recount His blessings and benefits.

We can let go of fear and doubt when, by faith, we receive the promises made by a Father who cannot lie. Our hearts can rest in peace and our souls can rejoice as we toss our seeds of faith into the honor and integrity of His Word. All His promises have been fulfilled in Christ Jesus, so we can give a resounding "Amen!" to each one. Our faith can be kept from wavering and find rest in the knowledge that the One who has promised is able to perform what He has spoken.

We can leave matters with God and refrain from worry when we are conscious of His continual presence. Growing in our awareness of the nearness of God is a constant source of comfort and strength.

We are kept by His omnipotence through our faith. Trusting and resting in Him is our victory. It is God's desire and glory that we dwell in the shadow of the Almighty enjoying the peace and joy He won for us on the cross. We are mutually blessed as we remain in His love and commune with Him in the shade of His presence.

Like an apple tree among the trees of the woods,
so is my beloved among the sons.
I sat down in his shade with great delight,
and his fruit was sweet to my taste.
he brought me to the banqueting house,
and his banner over me was love.
Song of Solomon 2:3–4

Recognize

Growing in the knowledge of His character and ability. What did you learn about God; His ability, plans, and purposes?

Remember

Recalling His blessings and benefits that you have experienced.

Receive

Has God reassured you with a promise this week?

Rest

In light of all you learned about God's character, ability, and promises, what are you able to release to His faithful care?

FLYING ARROW
ministries

More Books by Sher Pai

Be Still and know that I Am God. A 7 week study through Psalm 46.

Spanish, Be Still and know that I Am God. Estad Quietos y Conoced Que Yo Soy Dios. Un estudio Bíblico a través del Salmo 46.

Cultivating a Quiet Heart is a reflective and responsive journal created to compliment the Be Still Bible study.

Gifted for Service is an 8 week Bible study aimed at helping you discover your spiritual gifts.

Equipado Para Servir Descubriendo Su Dones Espirituales. Un estudio Bíblico para grupos.

Partners in Grace is a 15 week Bible study through the book of Philippians.

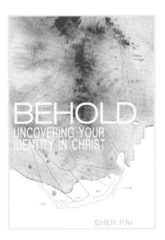

Behold is a Bible study with 16 chapters designed to help you uncover your true identity in Christ and challenge you to believe you are who God says you are.